Acknowledgment

Special thanks to those who encouraged me and stood with me throughout this endeavor: my husband Charlie Robinson, my children LaToya and Keldrick, my parents Marzetta & Wilson Nettles of Hybart Alabama, my Pastors Donald & Lucillie Ritchie, my Associate Pastors Henry & Annette Tate, my cousin Mrs. Ruh Young, and my best friend Lisa Blowe and family.

Contents

Dr. Martin Luther King Jr.

Dr. King was a man of courage,
one who rendered all of his service.

Dr. King was dedicated, honest and true,
one who fought to take his brothers through.

Dr. King was a man of average fame and
by no means was he ashamed.

Dr. King fought a very good fight,
and advised his people to hold on tight.

Dr. King was focused, a God sent angel,
one who realized his life was in danger.

Dr. King was a leader, and a quite sitter,
but one who was known to be no quitter.

Dr. M. L. King was a freedom fighter,
who knew that the future would be brighter.

He was the very best that we ever had,
so we know his soul is free at last!

4

My Burden Bearer

Who carries my burdens? not I or you,
but the living God who is fair and true.

Who carries my burdens? not the fortuneteller and
not the fairy, but a man who told me not to tarry.

Who carries my burdens? not mother or father,
but the prince of Peace, who is so kind hearted.

Who carries my burdens? not the president,
nor the governor, but a man who knows how to be a cover.
This man is Jesus, what a true pleaser!

Trouble Free

Look at me, I am trouble free;
because Jesus Christ lives in me.

Look at me, I am trouble free;
because he left all of my burden upon a tree.

Look at me, I am trouble free;
because Jesus Christ died for me.

Look at me, I am trouble free;
because I stay close to thee.

Look at me, I am trouble free;
because eternity is so dear to me.

Yes, I know that I am trouble free;
because "I'm on my way to heaven, you see."

I Had A Dream Last Night

I had a dream last night,
that I was rich and famous.

I had a dream last night
that I was living in danger.

I had a dream last night
that all my silver and gold were gone,
that someone came and stole my home.

I had a dream last night
that all the stars fell from heaven,
leaving me in the hands of the devil.

I had a dream last night that
a mighty rushing wind came in,
and tossed me from end to end.

Thank heaven when the nightmare ended.
It was wonderful to know this was just a dream!!

Making Preparation

I am making preparation for a higher plain.
I am making preparation for a spiritual gain.
I am making preparation for a home of gold,
one will keep my heavenly soul.

I am making preparation to reign on high,
far, far away beyond the sky.
I am making preparation for higher ground,
a place where I will go to wear a crown.

I am making preparation for a sin free life
one without pain, worry, or strife.

You need to prepare for a higher ground:
A place where you will wear a crown!

He Has Risen

Rejoice, Rejoice, Rejoice.
Pull off the old, put on the new.
Jesus Christ lives in you.

My Savior and your Lord has risen from the dead,
up from the grave; just like he said.

King of kings, Lord of Lords,
Prince of Peace, and the renewal of hearts.

Up from the grave, He lifted His head,
and God's children know they have nothing to dread.

Away rolled the stone where He lay,
away rolled all our fears and dismay.

The King is alive, the King is alive,
let your hearts rejoice inside.

Praise ye the Lord, praise ye the Lord.
Clap your hands; make a joyful noise!!

Christ has risen from the dead.
Yes, He has risen, just like he said.
Happy Easter!

What Is A Mother

A mother is friendship.
A mother is trust.

A mother is loyalty.
A mother is authority.

A mother is love that kind above.
A mother is a friend indeed, someone
to help you in times of need.

A mother is someone who cares and shares.
A mother is someone who is kind and true.
She will always see her child through.

A mother is kind-hearted, patient,
understanding, and loveable.
She will always be there in time of trouble.

A mother is someone who shows concern,
is full of laughter and lots of fun.

A mother is someone who will go her limit
To make sure her work is done, without blemish.
No matter how hard the task.

A mother will stand until the last.
A mother is as pure as gold.
She will watch out for her child's soul.

A mother is always true.
She will never forsake you.

Happy Mother's Day!

What is A Father?

A father is a comforter.
A father is strength.
A father is noble.
He's always sober.

A father is courage.
A father is guidance.

A father is a leader.
By no means is he a cheater.
A father is dependable.
He's a provider.
He's a helper.
He's a friend.
He has much strength that lies within.

A father is a man who fears God.
From his word, he will not depart.

A father is one who will take a task
and will stick to it until the last.

A father is one who will live right
and raise his children with all his might.

Fathers don't quit, and they certainly don't sit.
They will rise above tests and trials,
and will teach their children how to survive.

A father is understanding, honest, and fair, and will
trust in God and stay in prayer.

A father is one who will take a stand
and will do all that God commands.

Fathers, you are special in God's sight,
so keep up the good work, and fight, fight, fight!!!

Have a Happy Father's Day!

Drugs

Drugs, Drugs everywhere!
No one seems to care.

Drugs, drugs everywhere!
Who will take a stand and show that
You care?
Drugs in school; don't be fooled.

Drugs in homes;
they are even feeding it to the unborn.

Drugs in church;
who would think of such?

Drugs in prison,
which leads to bad mannerism.

Drugs in the street;
this one is hard to beat!

Drugs in the air;
this has left us beyond repair.

Drugs, Drugs everywhere!

Take a stand and do your share.
Take a stand and show that you care.

What My Dad Means To Me

My dad means the world and all.
Without him, I would be lost.

My dad is strong, patient, and smart.
He works hard, long, and fast.

My dad is a very good friend,
one whose love will never end.

My dad has a special touch,
and I love him very much.

My dad is a man of God.
From His word, he will not depart.

Dad, you mean the world and all.
Keep on working and standing tall.

Valentine's Day

Today is Valentine's Day.
What a happy feeling to be a precious valentine
on such a special day.

Valentines are hearts filled with love,
hearts that share pains, hearts that
share happiness, hearts that share joy,
and hearts that are full of sunshine forever more.

Oh, why don't you be my valentine, and
fill my heart with love, and bring
all the peace and happiness that only
one heart deserves?

A Christmas Star Is Shining

A Christmas star is shining,
high up in the sky,
guiding all the wise men and
shepherds to where the baby lies.

O, how beautiful the star is shining,
O, what good news it brings!!
Great tidings and peace to all
mankind forever and evermore.

O, little star, O, little star,
shine on, shine on, shine on.
May your joy, peace, and happiness
warm my heart forever, when I see
you there in our beautiful heaven.

My Church

Down the street and around a curve,
stands my church.

My church is small but loved by all.

My church is holy and very devoted.

My church stands on truth and will teach you
what to do.
My church is built on the Word of God,
and welcomes all, big and small.

There are no big I's and little U's.
We are all striving to make it through.

My church is true divine and teach its
people not to drink wine.

My church is a big cluster of love
and is willing to obey its God above.

Come and visit this little church;
we will love you very much.

My Pastors

My pastors are the dearest, loveable, and most
honest people that you can meet.

Pastors like mine are hard to beat.

They teach me things that I don't know.

They give me courage when I am feeling low.

They teach me how to will and do
and how to make my life anew.

They teach me how to hold on tight in
order that I will win this fight.

My pastors are ones who like to make friends
and will stand on God's word through thick and thin.

They are concerned, loving, and kind
and always keep the members in mind.

They treat each one of us the same
and love us all in Jesus name.

They are our friends;
they certainly don't pretend.
I thank my pastors for truth divine
and for how they teach us to pray for the blind.

To give to those in need,
for grace to help in thought and deed.

My pastors are a holy people
always willing to dig deeper.

I have the best
and will not settle for less.

So pastors, I will always love you.
You are kind-hearted and true.

No matter how the storm rage,
I know that you will continue with your crusade.

Gangs

Gangs are one of the most disgusting groups I have ever heard.
They try to rule this entire world.

Gangs are people who really don't care,
who are not willing do their share.

Gangs are people who are very cold hearted.
They're selfish, inhuman, and don't trust in God.

Gangs are people who hate themselves.
For sure, they will rebel.

Gangs are people who want to control by
doing crimes that have never been told.
They will kill, steal, mug, and rape.
There is no crime they will forsake.
They love jewels and fine cars.
What a shame they have no morals.
Kids, this is a group you must avoid.
For they will tear your life apart.
Keep yourself from this bunch called gangs.

For they are really insane.
Be a gang member for God.
For sure, your life will not fall apart.
Keep your eyes on Him above.
Show your fellowman some love.

Gangs, this is something that you might not know,
but you will reap whatever you sow!

God Is Always Near

Brothers and Sisters, there are often times
our lives are filled with troubles and fear,
because we're so easy to forget that
God is always near.

The wind will blow sometimes, and the storms
of life will rage; be joyful and full of cheer
because God is near.

Close your eyes to trouble and let your hearts rejoice.
We will win the battle if only we hear his voice.
The nights may grow longer; the sun may fade away.
Remember in Christ Jesus, there is always a better day!!

Stop being troubled by trouble.
Stop being worried by worrying.
Let us lift up His name, because we have everything to gain.
Stop being bound by fear; God is always near.

Heaven

Heaven is as beautiful as gold:
just waiting to be fill with precious souls.

Heaven is filled with pretty flowers:
encamped with angels and holy power.

Heaven is a holy place,
where we will see God face to face.

Heaven is a place of rest:
no more sorrow, but happiness.

Heaven is a place of peace,
where praises will never cease.

Heaven is a place of joy,
a place where the devil will never destroy.

Heaven is a place to shout,
a place where there will be no more doubt.

Heaven is a holy place,
where we will see God face to face!!

What Is A Family?

A family is a group of loving friends,
who will stick together through thick and thin.

They will share your joy and sorrow and will stand with you
until you are able to face tomorrow.

A family is one whose ties are strong; never will they leave you alone.
They will make sure your needs are met; they will not leave you alone to
fret.

A family is a blessing from God; from His word they should never depart.

A family is true and polite, striving to treat each other right.
They will not let hatred set in because they know the devil will win.
There will be disagreements, disappointments, and failures in all of us some-
times,
but a good family will not hold these things in mind; move forward and
forget the past,
and let your love for each other last.

A family is an everlasting bond, so let's enjoy each other and have fun.

Sowing And Reaping

There is a time to sow and time to reap,
believe it or not your sinful deeds will not just cease.

Sowing and reaping was designed by God,
Brothers and Sisters you better do your part.
Whatever you sow you are going to reap,
so His face is wise to seek.

Don't play games and expect no blame because
your deed will bring you shame. Some folks sow things
they dare to reap, but, Honey let me warn you,
your deeds will repeat.

Some folks sow evil and mess, try to deceive others
at their best. Some folks sow hurt and pain, but what
they don't know they are living in vain. Some folks sow
jealously, and division, but one day they will relive their decision.
Some folks sow joy and peace, and from giving God praises they will not
cease.
Some folks sow unity and love, and will serve their God above.

Some folks sow wisdom, and courage,
and to help those who are held captive by worry.

Remember these words, and watch what you sow,
for surely you want a spiritual crop to grow.

I Know A Man Who Never Gives Up

I know a man who never gives up:
a man of courage and plenty of success.

A man with a plan in his hands:
a man on top of all his demands.

I know a man who is full of fame;
he will turn your life into a living flame.

I know a man who is very polite;
shines like a noonday light.

I know a man who will make it to the top,
because he isn't going to be stopped.

Keep on working and doing your best.
Your life is sure to be a success!

Children Will Be Children

Children will be children,
regardless of what you say.
We, as Christian leaders,
must teach them how to pray.

Children will be children in their every play,
we, as Christian leaders, must keep
them from going astray.
Children will be children as soon as they are born,
we, as Christian leaders, must give them a holy home.

Children will be children as long as they breathe fresh air;
we, as Christian leaders, must show them that we care.

Children will be children until the days are done;
we, as Christian leaders, must never leave them alone.

Children will be children until Judgement Day;
please stop for a while and teach them how to pray.

A Tribute To My Parents

You are the most wonderful parents
that anyone could have.
You care for me in a special way;
your love grow stronger day by day.
You are as pure as gold, you are
always looking out for my soul.
You taught me things that were right
and never gave in to strife.
You sheltered me under your wings,
to help me fight off the devil's stings.
Your trust and loyalty I know well,
that's why I am standing to tell.
I love you with all my heart,
never to think depart.
I love you more than you could know,
I don't think I could ever let you go.
I am a part of you, forever,
to forget your love, never.
I love you more than words can say,
may God bless and keep you everyday.

The Virtuous Woman

One who stands bold and tall she's beautiful, soft spoken, brave, and bright,
one who stands for what is right. She's clever, she's pleasant,
she's warm and strong. She's one who will embrace the truth because she
realize that's what it takes to make it through.

The virtuous woman is honored by many because of her wisdom
is that of plenty.

The virtuous woman is righteous: she is pure as gold she always
thinking of her soul.

The virtuous woman is kind, honest, faithful, long suffering,
and patient because she knows she has to make it.

The virtuous woman is lovable; she knows how to withstand troubles.

The virtuous woman knows how to mend and to stay away from sin.

The virtuous woman takes care of her family, leaving all of her
work done without blemish. She cooks them good meals that flicker
their taste because this is her faithful race. She teaches her children
how to pray and give thanks to God everyday.

The virtuous woman walks and talks by faith; trusting in God to forgive
mistakes.

The virtuous woman is here to stay, to do God's will no matter what you
say.

Be a virtuous woman; for God's sake don't
let this be said, "too late!"

I Am A Bold Soldier

I am a bold soldier for my Lord.
Come rain, sleet, or snow, where he leads me I will go.

I am a bold soldier for my Lord.
Living holy and defeating the enemy this
will save the life of many.

I am a bold soldier for my Lord. Praying for the sick,
and sharing with the poor: these are things that I adore.

I am a bold soldier for my Lord standing
firmly on His word, and carrying the gospel to
those who haven't heard.

I am a bold soldier for my Lord. Winning souls is what I do best
and will not stop until God call me home to rest.
He that wins souls is wise, but living in sin God despises.

I am a bold soldier for my Lord. I will nurture my walk with God,
for He is the only one to keep me from falling a part.
I am a bold soldier for my Lord.

What is wrong with the world today?

What is wrong with the world today? People are living in such a
hurry. They are running to and fro, failing to find the right way to go.

What is wrong with the world today? People don't care about
one another; from God's word they are moving further.

What is wrong with world today? They are raping and killing the young
and the old, some stories haven't been told.

What is wrong with the world today? They are using drugs,
and drinking wine, and they think that the are living fine.

What is wrong with the world today? They are marrying and giving into
marriages; there is no time to tarry. They are robbing the church,
and stealing from the poor, so they will spend eternity in the pit below.

What is wrong with the world today? They are cheating,
procrastinating, and lying; these things will drive one out of their mind.
Teenage pregnancy is sky high, these are facts we can't deny.

What is wrong with the world today? Men are lovers of men, women are
lovers of women. What a shame for this generation have sins of many.
They are shacking up rather than marrying because this is a burden
some don't want to carry.

What is wrong with the world today? Well my friend, I give you some
answers: we have gone away from God, and sins of this world has torn us
apart; our steps are
not being ordered by God, because some say living holy is too hard.
We are not living a Godly life because we are fighting and living
in strife. We are not following God's holy plan, because we
feel that "I am the man." I am three times seven, and
then some more, no one can tell me to stay or go.
That's what is wrong with the world today.

In The Days of Old

In the days of old, things happened that were never told:
children were taken from their homes, beaten, and treated wrong.

My forefathers worked from dawn to dust;
in no one could they put their trust.
They cried to their master to give them a break,
oh, he would not listen for heaven's sake.

They used their talents to up lift their spirit as they worked
for their master so tired and weary.

They picked the cotton and hoed the fields,
but could not claim the fruit it yielded.

They worked in the rain, sleet, and snow,
because they had no place to go.

They prayed to God everyday,
because they knew He would make away.

They prayed hard as they worked,
while their clothes drench with sweat.

They shed many days of tears,
seeking God for old wounds to heal.

They sang songs of being heaven bound
when their old master wasn't around.

They sang songs of being free
to live their life happy, you see.

They told lots of funny jokes,
while they continued to cope.

They lived their lives in constant fear,
because they didn't know when their old master was n
They were afraid to speak out,
because that meant a whipping without a doubt.
They hung our forefathers from a tree.

These things happened in the days of old,
some things happened that weren't told.

Count Your Blessings

Count your blessings, give God praises,
give God thanks for the ways He made.

Count your blessings everyday,
and don't you ever forget to pray.

Count your blessings when things go wrong,
He will never leave you alone.

Count your blessing when you are down,
and you will never wear a frown.

Count your blessings everywhere you go;
you will surely receive more.

Count your blessings when times are bad;
God will never leave you sad.

Count your blessing in the time of need,
God will make sure you succeed.

Count your blessing and take a stand,
God will always lend a hand.

Homegoing

I am going home to be with my Lord.

I am moving to a place never to depart.

I am going to a place not made by hand.
This home was not made by man.

I am going to a home where I will not need a key.

I will be with the angels, and I'll be free.

I am going to a home where I won't need lights,

because of Jesus who shines so bright.

I am going to a home where all my bills are paid,
never to serve sin any more as a slave.

I am going home to a place made of gold,
it will keep and preserve my soul.

I am going home to a place of praise,
I will not be left in the grave.

I am going to a home that is far, far away.
May God keep and bless me everyday.
I am going home to be with my Lord, never more to part.

A Friend

A friend is a blessing indeed,
one who will be there in the time of need.

A friend is a blessing from God, one who
will show you love from his heart.

A friend is like an angel,
he will warn you of danger.

A friend is someone you can trust,
to have a true friend is a must.

A friend is more valuable than gold
because they can help make you whole.

A friend will show that he care
because he is always willing to share.

A friend will brighten up your day,
because he is special in every way.

A friend will always give you a smile,
just to see you laugh for a while.

A friend will keep you in mind;
he will help you through tough times.

A friend will stick like glue,
he will see you through.

A friend will stand from the beginning to the end.
There will come a time we all will need a friend.

A friend will stand through thick and thin,
and with a true friend you will always win.

What Is A Teacher?

A teacher is a friend indeed,
she will make sure you succeed.

A teacher is like a shining light,
she will teach you what is right.

A teacher will help you grow strong,
she will not lead you wrong.

A teacher is someone who is willing to guide,
she is always by your side.

A teacher is a mother away from home, she
refuse to let you just play and roam.

A teacher will encourage you to do your best,
so your life will be a success.

A teacher is someone you trust and love
because she was sent from heaven above.

A teacher is patient and kind,
because she knows that learning takes time.

A teacher is a gift from God;
to obtain her goal, she must work hard.

A War is Coming Upon This Land

A war is coming upon this land:
who shall be able to stand?

A war is coming upon this land,
you better start making your plans.

A war is coming upon this land,
no one will be able to lend a hand.

Your feet must not be planted on sinking sand.

A war is coming upon this land,
it will be stronger than any man.

A war is coming upon this land,
who shall be able to stand?

Why God Made Man?

God made man in his own image.
God made man perfect and without blemish.

God made man to give him glory,
to keep His word and live holy.

God made man to lead the way,
and to give Him praise everyday.

God made man to live free,
and not to take care of himself, you see.

God made man to be a light:
to shine both day and night.

God made man because He was lonely,
and to serve and obey Him only.

God made man to lean on His arms,
not to bring himself any harm.

God made man to take of this earth,
not to bring him shame and curse.

God made man in His own image.

God made man perfect and without blemish.

The House of God

The house of God is the House of Praise,
you should run to this place.

This Place is your training ground,
so you will be able to wear a crown.

The House of God is a Holy Place,
there; you learn to run this race.

The House of God is my protection;
this is where I receive directions,

This house was built with special care
for God's people to learn and share.

This house represents God,
come one, come all.

The House of God is a House of faith,
you should attend; you shouldn't wait.

This house will deny no one,
no matter where you are from.

The House of God is a Place of Worship;
keep the faith and keep on pushing.

Prayer

Prayer is strength in the time of sorrow;
it will help you face tomorrow.

Prayer is a heart fixer and mind regulator.
What can make you feel greater?

Pray in the morning noon, and night.
PRAY, PRAY, PRAY with all your might.

Prayer is fellowshipping and communicating with God.
Keep your line open and from His Word you shall
never depart.

Prayer is good for the soul;
be wise and pray loud and bold.

Pray in the morning, noon and night.

PRAY, PRAY, PRAY with all your might.

Stay Connected

Stay connected to the Word of God,
share it with one and all.

Stay connected to God's power;
pray for this world every hour.

Stay connected to God's love,
obey Him and praise His son above.

Stay connected to God's Peace,
share it with others and don't let it cease.

Stay connected with God's plan;
obey Him and not man.

Stay connected with the Tree of Life,
so you will not live in strife.

Stay connected with God's Saints,
and don't be caught with those that ain't.

Stay connected to the Prince of Peace,
you will win all of your battles, you see.

Stay connected with prayer,
so when you need Him, He will be there.

Stay connected until the sun goes down,
He promised you would wear a crown.

Stay connected until Judgement Day;
don't let nothing get in your way.

God's Plan

God gave us His Holy Plan,
He entrusted it in the hands of man.

God gave us His Plan to live holy,
to serve Him and be devoted.

God gave us His Plan to win souls,
never to compromise for silver or gold.

God gave us His Plan to lead us from earth
to glory, you must stay sober and follow it boldly.

God gave us His plan to always win,
and never to be a slave to sin.

God gave us His Plan to love, to obey His word,
and trust Him above.

God gave us His Plan to take care of this land,
and feed His people at His command.

God gave us His Plan to walk upright,
to let our light shine both day and night.

God gave us His Plan to forgive,
to destroy evil, and don't let it live.

God gave us His Plan to conquer all,
without this plan, we all would fall.

Seek this plan follow it boldly,
you will always remain sober.

This plan is the Holy Bible.

Christmas Time

Christmas is a time to share;
to show someone that you care.

Christmas is the birth of Christ,
who died for our sins and strife.

Christmas is a time of giving,
to show someone else life is worth living.

Christmas is a time of praise,
to give God thanks for how He saves.

Christmas is a time for fun,
for children to jump, play, and run.

Christmas is a time of celebration,
there is no time for separation.

Enjoy yourself and remember
Christ the One who saved our life.

Have a Merry Christmas
and a Happy New Year!

Lean On Me.

Lean on me when things go wrong,
you won't have to suffer alone.

Lean on me when you are down and out,
I will be there, without a doubt.

Lean on me in the times of trouble,
I will be there on the double.

Lean on me when your friends are gone,
I will never leave you alone.

Lean on me when you are weak,
I am the One you need to seek.

Lean on me when you are sick,
I am the healer you need to pick.

Lean on me when all has failed,
I am the only one that can prevail.

Lean on me through your test and trials:
sit and rest for a while.

Lean on me everyday,
I will surely make a way.

Lean on me from dawn to dust,
I am the one you need to trust.

Lean on me when things go wrong
you want have to suffer alone.

The Characteristics of a Black Woman

A black woman is clever; she is wise
and she knows how to survive.

A black woman is smart;
she set her goals and she works hard.

A black woman is patient;
and she is hard to yield to temptation.

A black woman is strong;
she teaches her children right from wrong.

A black woman is sexy and beautiful,
takes care of family and is very dutiful.

A black woman is a woman of vision,
she always makes wise decisions.

A black woman has a love for God,
she has His word hidden in her heart.

A black woman is a woman of wisdom;
listen to her take on her mannerism.

A black woman is a woman of many talents:
she cooks, she cleans, it doesn't matter.

A black woman is a woman you can't predict,
if you think so you've been tricked.

A black woman doesn't play around,
wrong her, and she will knock you flat on the ground.

A black woman will speak out; this the truth without a doubt.
A black woman is a woman who needs no boost, she can show you how to get loose.
A black woman is a woman of courage; she will take time; she's in no hurry.
A black woman tries to do right, don't push her because she will fight.

A black woman is basically good; just don't mess around in her "hood."

Last and Evil Days

We are living in evil days,
people are doing everything except giving God praise.

People are robbing, killing, and stealing;
they don't care about anyone's feelings.

This world is turning upside down;
everywhere you look people are wearing a frown.

We are living in the last days.
It is time to change our ways.

People are turning to violence and drugs;
they are doing things you never heard.

They are using others more than ever;
they don't care about going to heaven.

People are doing wrong on every hand,
they have forgotten about God's command.

People are busy going to and fro;
they don't believe you will reap what you sow.

Keep on living and obeying this flesh,
you are going to find yourself in a mess.

If you don't listen to the Word of God,
your life is sure to fall a part.

Our teenagers are gone astray,
because of our bad living from day to day.

People don't care about you nor me;
you better strive to set yourself free.

They are down right mean;
they don't care about living clean.
In these last and evil days you better strive to change your ways.

The Integrity of a Black Man

A black man is strong and noble; he is kind and sober.
A black man is a man who needs a special touch:
just to know he is loved means so much.

A black man is a man with a strong will:
love him and help him heal.
A black man is a man of courage:
show him respect or move in a hurry.

A black man is a man who doesn't like to be teased,
yet sweet and easy to please.
A black man is a man of power;
treat them right or they will sour.

A black man is a man who works hard
to make sure his family doesn't fall apart.
A black man is a man who is tough,
he doesn't play he is rough.

A black man is a man who doesn't take mess,
if you don't believe this, put him to the test.
A black man is a man who will fight,
those that bother him are not very bright.

A black man is a man who can take care of his own.
You better mind your business and leave him alone.
A black man is a man who will lend a helping hand,
band together, and take a stand.
A black man is a man with a plan,
follow his lead as God command.

A black man is a man who needs much prayer;
love him and show him that you care.
A black man is the right man for you to meet,
his love and kindness is hard to beat.

A black man is a man who has lots of fun,
don't destroy him and call him a bum.
Give our black men a salute,
because they just need a boost.

Whom Shall I call?

Whom shall I call when I am sinking low
and don't know which way to go?

When I feel there is no hope, whom can I call for support?
When all of my friend are gone, and I am left all alone.
Whom shall I call?

When my heart is racing with fear, and there is no one near.
Whom shall I call?

When my body is filled with pain and I feel there is nothing to gain.
Whom shall I call?

When there is no peace in my home, and seem like everything has gone
wrong.
Whom shall I call?

When my life has turned up side down and my face is filled with frowns.
Whom shall I call?

When I feel my prayers are not heard, and everything seems to get on my
nerve.
Whom shall I call?

When all doors have been closed in my face, and I have no hiding place.
Whom shall I call?

When the brightest cloud has turned dark and I don't know where to start.
Whom shall I call?

When I am at my lowest point, and there is no time to front.
Whom shall I call?

I have learned to call on that Rock: the one who will give me a strong prop.
I have learned to call on my Savior; the One who I know is able.

I learn to call on the Prince of Peace to give Him praise, I will not cease.

I have learned to call on Jesus the One who is a True Pleaser.

Don't Tell Me What I Already Know

Don't tell me what I already know;
tell me something that will make me glow.

Don't tell me what I already know;
tell me something that will help me to grow.

Don't tell me what I already know;
tell me I am going to reap what I sow.

Don't tell me what I already know;
tell me of all the good things I have in store.

Don't tell me what I already know;
tell me how to let the God in me show.

Don't tell me what I already know;
tell me how to receive blessings galore!

Don't tell me what I already know;
tell me how to stay on the go.

Don't tell me what I already know;
tell me how to give to receive more.

Don't tell me what I already know;
tell me how to let my love flow.

Don't tell me what I already know;
tell me something to help me grow.

A Woman of Class

A woman of class would say, "check out my past."
I am sexy, beautiful, and classy.
I am wonderful and full of passion.
I am your today, I am your tomorrow, I am your future.

I am a woman of class.
I am not about mess, I am the best, and I will pass all of my tests!!

I am a woman of class. This is no charade,
I need some aid, and then your love will not fade.

I am a woman of class. I am bad, I will make you glad, but
please don't make me mad.

I am a woman of class.
I am fine, I don't drink wine, and I am on my own time.
I am a woman of class. Take care of your home, leave mine alone,
and don't call me to gossip on my phone.

I am a woman of class.
What you see is what you get, you better move very quick
because these words you can't forget.

I am a woman of class.
I stay on the go getting ready for the next blow,
don't take me fast; take me slow.

I am a woman of class. I obey no man I have my own
plan, and I will move by my own demand.

I am a woman of class. I am it I can't afford to get bit,
and if I do my time with you, I will split.

I am a woman of class. Don't play me for a fool,
I am not your tool, but if you think so you are not very cool.

I am a woman of class. I am rough; I am tough,
and I really don't take no stuff.

I am a woman of class. I am great; I am never late
and you love to take me on a date.

I am a woman of class.
I will rock your world, throw you some curves
and whisper you some sweet words you have never heard.
I am a woman of class.

Notes

Notes